Right where you are. That's where God will meet you. I'm praying you experience His love in your life today!

Do not despise these small beginnings, for the L*ORD* *rejoices to see the work begin.*

ZECHARIAH 4:10 NLT

"Little things" have big potential with God.

Rich Davis

DaySpring

For more
inspiration,
scan here:

You are a beautiful soul and an amazing human. I'm praying you know it deeply today.

Thank You for making me so
wonderfully complex!
Your workmanship is marvelous—
how well I know it.

PSALM 139:14 NLT

God sees us as we are, loves us as we are, and accepts us as we are. But by His grace, He does not leave us as we are.

Timothy Keller

Praying for you today. I don't have all the answers (or even most of them!), but we can discover Jesus together, anytime you want.

If you confess with your mouth that Jesus is Lord and believe in your heart that God raised him from the dead, you will be saved.

ROMANS 10:9 ESV

Every single person on this planet has been called to say yes to Jesus. To love, follow, and obey Him. It's like God sent out a group text to the whole world because "He does not want anyone to be lost" (II Peter 3:9 NCV).

Sadie Robertson

DaySpring

For more
inspiration,
scan here:

I want you to experience God's love to the fullest, because it will utterly change your life. I'm asking God to show you His love in a big way.

What no eye has seen, what no ear has heard, and what no human mind has conceived—the things God has prepared for those who love Him—these are the things God has revealed to us by His Spirit.

I CORINTHIANS 2:9–10 NIV

Yesterday is behind you;
tomorrow is out of reach.
Today is an unexplored treasure
with adventures waiting.

Lisa Stilwell

DaySpring

For more
inspiration,
scan here:

It's hard to choose joy and hope in hard times. But I'm in this with you, and I'm praying you discover the greatest treasures of God in the midst of it all.

For the LORD *your God is living among you. He is a mighty savior. He will take delight in you with gladness. With His love, He will calm all your fears. He will rejoice over you with joyful songs.*

ZEPHANIAH 3:17 NLT

The secret to joy is to keep seeking God where we doubt He is.

Ann Voskamp

I'm praying that you will see yourself and your situation the way God does—with grace, hope, and so much love.

And God saw everything that he had made, and behold, it was very good.

GENESIS 1:31 ESV

Don't look back at your mistakes and let them decide your future. God can still absolutely, 100 percent use you. He is just that good.

Sadie Robertson

DaySpring

For more
inspiration,
scan here:

It takes faith to believe that Jesus is who He says He is, and that wager is so very worth it. I'm praying you experience Him in undeniable ways.

Jesus said to her, "I am the resurrection and the life. He who believes in Me, though he may die, he shall live."

JOHN 1:14 NKJV

Jesus has been and will always be more than enough.

Karina Allen

DaySpring

For more inspiration, scan here:

You are such an important person in God's eyes. He wants to partner with you for good. I'm praying that you see your dreams fulfilled in Him and your heart delighted by Him.

Surely God is good . . .
to those who are pure in heart.

PSALM 73:1 NIV

Every day God invites us on the same kind of adventure. It's not a trip where He sends us a rigid itinerary; He simply invites us. God asks what it is He's made us to love, what it is that captures our attention, what feeds that deep indescribable need of our souls to experience the richness of the world He made. And then, leaning over us, He whispers, "Let's go do that together."

Bob Goff

For more inspiration, scan here:

Whatever you're carrying is not too heavy for God. I'm praying that you will be able to leave your burdens at His feet and experience what true rest feels like.

Give your burdens to the LORD,
and He will take care of you.
PSALM 55:22 NLT

God hears our prayers.
He knows the desires of our hearts.
He understands our deepest longings.
We will never be overlooked or forgotten.
Holley Gerth

DaySpring

For more
inspiration,
scan here:

I'm asking God to wrap you in His arms and show you the way to true peace.

Be joyful. Grow to maturity.
Encourage each other.
Live in harmony and peace.
Then the God of love and peace will be with you.

II CORINTHIANS 13:11 NLT

It is always more of Jesus that changes the world.
It is never because we are great or that we improve;
it is because we surrendered and He saves.

Cleere Cherry

DaySpring

For more inspiration, scan here:

Believe it or not, God wants you to flourish. That's why He wants you to know His Son. I'm praying that you thrive and be blessed in every way.

You shall rejoice in all the good that the LORD *your God has given to you and to your house.*

DEUTERONOMY 26:11 ESV

God's strength makes us strong;
His comfort comforts us.
With Him, we no longer run; we rest.

Dillon Burroughs

DaySpring

For more inspiration, scan here:

It's hard to comprehend how amazing God is and what He can do in and for us. I'm asking Him to show you clear direction and glimmering hope.

He who is mighty has done great things for me, and holy is *His name.*

LUKE 1:49 NKJV

You don't have to have all the answers.
If you put your faith and trust in God,
He will guide you toward the right decisions.

Maghon Taylor

I'm praying that as you grow in Jesus, you thoroughly enjoy the process of seeing Him work in your life in surprising and wonderful ways.

To them God has chosen to make known among the Gentiles the glorious riches of this mystery, which is Christ in you, the hope of glory.

COLOSSIANS 1:27 NIV

Give Him your mess and let it become your message.

Joyce Meyer

No matter where you are, if you choose to trust God, you can always look ahead with anticipation at what He is up to. I'm asking Him to give you a glimpse of His plans today!

This is what the LORD *says . . .*
"See, I am doing a new thing!
Now it springs up."
ISAIAH 43:16, 19 NIV

God is doing something new on a regular basis.
God is doing something new every day.
Joyce Meyer

God has His eye on you. He cares so deeply for you. And for every tiny step you take in His direction, He leaps toward you. I'm praying you feel His big, warm hugs today.

Be strong and courageous!
Do not be afraid or discouraged.
For the LORD your God is with you
wherever you go.
JOSHUA 1:9 NLT

The earth has no sorrow
that heaven cannot heal.
Thomas Moore

It doesn't take much, friend. Just the tiniest faith that God is who He says He is and that He keeps His promises. He can work miracles with that. I'm praying for you today.

*Let your roots grow down into Him,
and let your lives be built on Him. Then your faith
will grow strong in the truth you were taught,
and you will overflow with thankfulness.*

COLOSSIANS 2:7 NLT

Nothing is more dangerous, more compelling, more freeing, more radical, more real, more satisfying, more powerful than a person holding a smidgen of faith.

Jennie Allen

DaySpring

For more inspiration, scan here:

If it's peace your heart longs for, Jesus—the Prince of Peace—is the One your heart needs. Know that I'm praying for you and asking God to bring you His incredible peace.

In peace I will lie down and sleep,
for you alone, LORD, make me dwell in safety.

PSALM 4:8 NIV

As soon as we start to find our strength in God and His Word, worry fades, and faith takes charge.

Candace Cameron Bure

DaySpring

For more inspiration, scan here:

Choosing Jesus doesn't mean there won't be storms, but there will be hope in the midst of them. In dark times, there will be a light. I'm asking God to be present for you today.

And we know that God causes everything to work together for the good of those who love God and are called according to His purpose for them.

ROMANS 8:28 NLT

The good life isn't the absence of heartache; it's the presence of God, by grace, in the midst of it. Our hope in the midst of hardship is that Jesus doesn't just work things out for our good—He is our good.

Ruth Chou Simons

DaySpring

For more
inspiration,
scan here:

God loves you so much. I'm asking Him to tenderly show you His care in a way that is special and personal to you.

"Peace I leave with you;
my peace I give to you.
Not as the world gives do I give to you.
Let not your hearts be troubled,
neither let them be afraid."

JOHN 14:27 ESV

There is no pit so deep that
God's love is not deeper still.

Corrie ten Boom

Do you know what God's love feels like? I'm praying that it would be unmistakable for you today.

The LORD *is good to all, and His tender mercies are over all His works.*

PSALM 145:9 NKJV

He longs to quiet your heart with His love, to calm your fears, insecurities, and doubts with His presence.

Renee Swope

For more inspiration, scan here:

I'm asking God to reveal His purpose for you today. You are chosen, seen, and loved!

There is a time for everything,
and a season for every activity
under the heavens.

ECCLESIASTES 3:1 NIV

Just think . . . you're here not by chance, but by God's choosing. His hand formed you and made you the person you are. He compares you to no one else—you are one of a kind. You lack nothing that His grace can't give you. He has allowed you to be here at this time in history to fulfill His special purpose for this generation.

Roy Lessin

God loves you so much, and He wants so much for you. I'm praying that your purpose feels clear and strong today—you were made for this!

"You are precious to Me. You are honored, and I love you."

ISAIAH 43:4 NLT

You are here for a reason. Your life is part of a plan. You were placed here on purpose for a purpose.

Max Lucado

You don't have to earn anything with God; you only have to believe. I'm praying that His love is very real to you today.

See what kind of love the Father has given to us, that we should be called children of God; and so we are.

1 JOHN 3:1 ESV

Saving us is the greatest and most concrete demonstration of God's love, the definitive display of His grace throughout time and eternity.

David Jeremiah

It takes courage to believe in Jesus, and to tell others that you do. But He believes in you too. I'm praying for you today.

It is by believing in your heart that you are made right with God, and it is by openly declaring your faith that you are saved.

ROMANS 10:10 NLT

Grace is the free, undeserved goodness and favor of God to mankind.

Matthew Henry

DaySpring

For more
inspiration,
scan here:

Asking God to give you a taste of His goodness today. He has no shortage of goodness waiting for you!

The boundary lines have fallen
for me in pleasant places;
surely I have a delightful inheritance.

PSALM 16:6 NIV

There is no promise too hard for God to fulfill.
No prayer is too big for Him to answer!

Christine Caine

God knows where you struggle and what you long for most. I'm asking Him to show you how much He cares today.

And God is able to bless you abundantly,
so that in all things at all times,
having all that you need,
you will abound in every good work.

II CORINTHIANS 9:8 NIV

Everything you need, God already is.

Priscilla Shirer

For more
inspiration,
scan here:

It takes courage to pray and trust God with the answers. But He knows that, and He longs for you to know how much you matter to Him. I'm asking God to answer your prayers today in a big way.

The prayer of a person living right with God is something powerful to be reckoned with.

JAMES 5:16 THE MESSAGE

There is no force on earth stronger or more effective than the power of praying to our all-knowing, almighty God.

Linn Carlson

No one loves you more than Jesus does. I'm praying you sense His incredible mercy and grace toward you today.

"Greater love has no one than this, that someone lay down his life for his friends."

JOHN 15:13 ESV

The dearest friend on earth is a mere shadow compared to Jesus Christ.

Oswald Chambers

Asking God to hold out His hand to you today. If you take it, you will never, ever regret it.

You will show me the path of life;
in Your presence is fullness of joy;
at Your right hand are pleasures forevermore.

PSALM 16:11 NKJV

As we walk with Jesus,
He brings healing to our souls.

Becky Hastings

For more inspiration, scan here:

Every day with God is a good one. I'm praying you have that kind of day, a day in which you know beyond a shadow of a doubt how close He is and how much He loves you.

This is the day the LORD *has made. We will rejoice and be glad in it.*

PSALM 118:24 NLT

The long way around with God is a lot better than the shortcut without God.

Christine Caine

God invites us to lay down our burdens and trust Him to carry us through. Today I am praying that for you.

"Come to Me, all you who are weary and burdened, and I will give you rest."

MATTHEW 11:28 NIV

When you carry the weight of yesterday, it will ruin the power of today and the progress of tomorrow.

Tony Evans

DaySpring

For more
inspiration,
scan here:

I'm praying that today you get a glimpse of how much you matter to God.

How precious to me
are your thoughts, O God!
How vast is the sum of them!
If I would count them,
they are more than the sand.

PSALM 139:17–18 ESV

God is the only One who has the authority to tell you who you are.

Sarah Mae

I believe in you, and God does too. I'm asking Him to walk hand in hand with you through the journey you're on.

Anyone who believes in Him
will never be put to shame.

ROMANS 10:11 NIV

Putting the pieces of your broken life back together takes work. No matter what you did, no matter who let you down, you can always run to Him. This doesn't mean life will immediately be easy. But Jesus sees our rawness, brokenness, and fear. And He loves us anyway. We don't have to face it alone.

Candace Cameron Bure

For more
inspiration,
scan here:

I see a spark in you that God can ignite. I see a light in you that wants to shine so brightly. I'm praying for you today, believing the very best for your future!

The LORD always keeps His promises;
He is gracious in all He does.

PSALM 145:13 NLT

Your future is as bright as the promises of God.

William Carey

Nothing impacts our lives more than when we understand how much God wants us as part of His family. I'm praying you experience His joy today.

Let your steadfast love, O LORD, be upon us,
even as we hope in you.

PSALM 33:22 ESV

I believed that there was a God because I was told it
by my grandmother and later by other adults.
But when I found that I knew not only that there was
God but that I was a child of God, when I understood that,
when I comprehended that—more than that—
when I internalized that, ingested that,
I became courageous.

Maya Angelou

When we say yes to Jesus, we can be sure that what lies ahead is way better than anything left behind. I'm asking God to give you a taste of the excitement and joy of believing in Him today!

Now faith is the substance of things hoped for, the evidence of things not seen.

HEBREWS 11:1 NKJV

God already knows every single thing that every minute of every hour of every week of every month of this year will hold for you.

Elisabeth Elliot

DaySpring

For more
inspiration,
scan here:

There's no greater gift than belonging to God. I'm asking Him to assure you in your fears, comfort you in trouble, and give you peace like you've never had before.

Thanks be to God for His indescribable gift!

II CORINTHIANS 9:15 NIV

God doesn't just give us grace;
He gives us Jesus, the Lord of Grace.

Joni Eareckson Tada

For more inspiration, scan here:

Trusting is so hard, but there is truly no greater payoff. I'm praying that for even the smallest hope you give to Him, you receive His love and grace in amazing abundance.

Blessed is the one who trusts in the LORD.

PSALM 40:4 NIV

When we are on the beach, we only see a small part of the ocean. However, we know that there is much more beyond the horizon.

Corrie ten Boom

I'm praying for you today, asking for God's blessing over your life, and believing Him for everything He promised you in Jesus.

Blessed be the God and Father of our Lord Jesus Christ, who has blessed us in Christ with every spiritual blessing in the heavenly places.

EPHESIANS 1:3 ESV

Many of us are missing something in life because we are after the second best. I put before you what I have found to be the best—One who is worthy of all our devotion—Jesus Christ. He is the Savior for the young and the old.

Eric Liddell

DaySpring

For more inspiration, scan here:

I want the very best for you, friend, and that means wanting Jesus to overwhelm you with His love and generous grace. I'm praying for you today!

Delight yourself also in the LORD,
and He shall give you the desires of your heart.

PSALM 37:4 NKJV

Through Jesus, your past is explained,
your present has a purpose, and your future is secure.
What more could you really want in life?

Jase Robertson

DaySpring

For more
inspiration,
scan here:

Jesus changes everything. When you're in pain, He's your Comforter. When you're afraid, He's your Deliverer. He fills you with hope when you're empty. I'm praying you come to know Him fully.

"I have come that they may have life, and have it to the full."

JOHN 10:10 NIV

Jesus came for us so that we might come to Him.
He emptied Himself so that we might be filled with His fullness.
He became a servant so that we might be made His heirs.
He wore a crown of thorns so that we might wear a crown of glory.

Sheryl L. Kelly

God wants more for you than you could ever imagine, and He can do it! Praying you see Him at work on your behalf.

May He grant your heart's desires and make all your plans succeed.

PSALM 20:4 NLT

Our confidence comes from believing God can do anything, then stepping back and letting Him.

Jennie Allen

DaySpring

For more
inspiration,
scan here:

Saying yes to Jesus means experiencing love like you never have before. Praying you will feel His big, big love today.

The love of God has been poured out in our hearts.

ROMANS 5:5 NKJV

Just think about how much God loves us! God never has to ask us what we're thinking about. He knows our hopes and desires, our aspirations and dreams. He loves us.

Thelma Wells

For more inspiration, scan here:

Following Jesus is not a life sentence; it is a life-bringing joy. I'm praying for brighter, bolder days ahead for you!

But the path of the just is like the shining sun, that shines ever brighter unto the perfect day.

PROVERBS 4:18 NKJV

Abide in Me, says Jesus. Cling to Me.
Stick fast to Me. Live the life of close and intimate
communion with Me. Get nearer to Me.
Roll every burden on Me. Cast your whole weight on Me.
Never let go your hold on Me for a moment.
Be, as it were, rooted and planted in Me. Do this and I will
never fail you. I will ever abide in you.

J.C. Ryle

DaySpring

For more inspiration, scan here:

It's a choice that only you get to make. But when you do, your heart will thrive like never before. I'm praying you discover true strength and hope very soon.

But those who hope in the L*ORD will renew their strength. They will soar on wings like eagles; they will run and not grow weary, they will walk and not be faint.*

ISAIAH 40:31 NIV

He who created us without our help will not save us without our consent.

Augustine

For more inspiration, scan here:

I'm asking God to show you how very much He loves you.

God showed how much
He loved us by sending
His one and only Son into the world
so that we might have eternal life through Him.

I JOHN 4:9 NLT

Christ must always be an open door
with a welcome sign for all.

Johnny Cash

God is good,
all the time.
I'm praying you
feel His goodness
in life-changing
ways today.

For the LORD is good;
his steadfast love endures forever,
and his faithfulness to all generations.

PSALM 100:5 ESV

You're born. You suffer. You die.
Fortunately, there's a loophole.

Billy Graham

May God's gifts of hope, peace, and promise be yours today. Praying for you!

Every good gift and every perfect gift is from above, and comes down from the Father of lights, with whom there is no variation or shadow of turning.

JAMES 1:17 NKJV

My deepest awareness of myself is that I am deeply loved by Jesus Christ and I have done nothing to earn it or deserve it.

Brennan Manning

For more inspiration, scan here:

Jesus came so that you would have hope beyond measure and peace beyond reason. I'm praying for you!

She will give birth to a son,
and you are to give Him the name Jesus,
because He will save His people from their sins.

MATTHEW 1:21 NIV

Through salvation our past has
been forgiven, our present is
given meaning, and our future is secured.

Rick Warren

I'm praying for you, believing with all my heart that God is the answer to everything you need.

"Be still, and know that I am God!"

PSALM 46:10 NLT

God is to problems what a hurricane is to a mosquito. No match.

Max Lucado

Asking God to meet your needs in a way that overwhelms and blesses you. He can do it!

Your Father knows what you need before you ask him.

MATTHEW 6:8 ESV

When we begin to realize that we have so little to offer is when we can begin to realize how much God has to give.

Roy Lessin

For more inspiration, scan here:

No one can understand you like Jesus can. I'm praying you feel His loving comfort today.

The LORD is near to those
who have a broken heart,
and saves such as have a contrite spirit.

PSALM 34:18 NKJV

In the midst of the storm,
Jesus is the only One who can bring peace.

Jill Kelly

DaySpring

For more
inspiration,
scan here:

Did you know that Jesus is the Prince of Peace? I'm praying you experience His kind of peace today.

Grace and peace to you from God our Father and the Lord Jesus Christ.

PHILEMON 1:3 NIV

No one can have the peace of God until they are at peace with God.

Jack Wellman

Jesus gave everything because of His love for us. I'm praying you feel loved today, in the deepest way.

"For this is how God loved the world: He gave His one and only Son, so that everyone who believes in Him will not perish but have eternal life."

JOHN 3:16 NLT

When you go after something you love, you'll do anything it takes to get it, even if it costs everything.

Bob Goff

I'm asking God to meet your every need today, and praying you recognize His loving gifts.

The LORD will give strength to His people; the LORD will bless His people with peace.

PSALM 29:11 NKJV

God is faithful. He'll fulfill every promise He's made. There's no disease God cannot heal, no heart He cannot mend, no bondage He cannot break, no enemy He cannot defeat, no mountain He cannot move, no need He cannot meet.

Christine Caine

I thanked God for you today.

I thank my God in all my remembrance of you

PHILIPPIANS 1:3 ESV

It is not how much we have but
how much we enjoy that makes happiness.

Charles Spurgeon

For more
inspiration,
scan here:

Despite what people sometimes think, believing in Jesus is quite wonderful. And I wouldn't be a friend if I didn't want that joy for you. So I'm praying for you today.

May the God of hope fill you with all joy and peace in believing.

ROMANS 15:13 NKJV

Hope is ours for the taking every single minute. It's the assurance that things will make sense when there's no sense to make of things.

Luci Swindoll

For more
inspiration,
scan here:

Whatever is holding you back today, I'm praying you feel the freedom to move forward in faith. God will meet you there.

The Lord will indeed give what is good,
and our land will yield its harvest.

PSALM 85:12 NIV

Don't be afraid to step out and trust God.
He is more faithful than the rising of the sun.

Kari Jobe

Praying that God would answer your prayers and fulfill your deepest desires.

God can do anything, you know—
far more than you could ever imagine or
guess or request in your wildest dreams!
He does it not by pushing us around but
by working within us, His Spirit
deeply and gently within us.

EPHESIANS 3:20 THE MESSAGE

Without Jesus we face a hopeless end,
but with Jesus we have an endless hope.

Barbara Johnson

DaySpring

For more
inspiration,
scan here:

I'm praying for you today, longing for you to see Him bless your heart.

Love bears all things,
believes all things,
hopes all things,
endures all things.
Love never ends.

1 CORINTHIANS 13:7–8 ESV

Be assured that there is no sin you have ever committed that the blood of Jesus Christ cannot cleanse.

Billy Graham

DaySpring

For more
inspiration,
scan here:

Trusting God can seem scary at times, but it is always the right decision. I'm praying you find the courage to trust Him with everything you need.

Trust in the LORD *with all your heart,*
and lean not on your own understanding;
in all your ways acknowledge Him,
and He shall direct your paths.

PROVERBS 3:5–6 NKJV

God never calls a person [into His service] without equipping him. I know that from experience.

Billy Graham

What do you need most today? Entrust it to God, and He will answer, every time. I'm praying for you!

The LORD always keeps His promises;
He is gracious in all He does.

PSALM 145:13 NLT

If the Lord be with us, we have no cause for fear.
His eye is upon us, His arm over us,
His ear open to our prayer, His grace sufficient,
His promise unchangeable.

John Newton

I'm praying for you today. The more you choose to hand over to God, the more He has to work with—and the more miracles He can work on your behalf.

I pray that you, being rooted and established in love, may have power, together with all the Lord's holy people, to grasp how wide and long and high and deep is the love of Christ.

EPHESIANS 3:17–18 NIV

May you always be rooted in the soil of God's love.

Max Lucado

You are a true treasure to God and to me. I'm praying you know that deep down today.

"I know what I am planning for you," says the LORD.
"I have good plans for you, not plans to hurt you.
I will give you hope and a good future."

JEREMIAH 29:11 NCV

God's plan for your life is as special
as the person He created in you.

Bonnie Rickner Jensen

For more inspiration, scan here:

God loves you so much! He created you for a purpose. And I'm praying you can receive that gift today, knowing that His plans for you are so good.

See how very much our Father loves us.

1 JOHN 3:1 NLT

It is wonderful to know that God is love, but it is even more wonderful to know that He loves you.

Roy Lessin

Today I'm asking God to wrap you in His warm embrace and show you the way to lasting peace.

Then the angel said to them, "Do not be afraid, for behold, I bring you good tidings of great joy which will be to all people. For there is born to you this day in the city of David a Savior, who is Christ the Lord."

LUKE 2:10–11 NKJV

Emmanuel. God with us. He who resided in heaven, coequal and coeternal with the Father and the Spirit, willingly descended into our world. He breathed our air, felt our pain, knew our sorrows, and died for our sins. He didn't come to frighten us, but to show us the way to warmth and safety.

Chuck Swindoll

For more inspiration, scan here:

Do you have any idea how amazing you are? How loved and wanted you are? I'm praying you do.

"For I know the plans I have for you,"
says the LORD. *"They are plans for good . . .*
to give you a future and a hope."

JEREMIAH 29:11 NLT

Each one of us has a purpose in the Lord.

Stormie Omartian

For more
inspiration,
scan here:

You are a beautiful part of this world, handcrafted by God for a specific purpose. I'm praying you truly taste His goodness today, knowing that you are meant to be a part of it.

Taste and see that the LORD is good.
Oh, the joys of those who take refuge in Him!

PSALM 34:8 NLT

Everything beautiful begins with God.

Bonnie Rickner Jensen

DaySpring

For more
inspiration,
scan here:

There's no limit to what God can do when you give Him the reins of your life. I'm praying you see Him at work in your life today, tomorrow, and every day after that.

May He give you the desire of your heart and make all your plans succeed.

PSALM 20:4 NIV

We often can't see what God is doing in our lives, but God sees the whole picture and His plan for us clearly.

Tony Dungy

It's hard to understand the depth of commitment God has toward you, but you can find that answer in Jesus. He went all the way. I'm praying you grasp His love for you in a big way.

In Your hand is power and might;
in Your hand it is *to make*
great and to give strength to all.
I CHRONICLES 29:12 NKJV

Most people wouldn't give their only begotten French fry, yet God gave His Son. Quite frankly, that's impressive.
Keion Jackson

Jesus loves you unconditionally. Today I'm praying your heart knows it, believes it, and receives Him.

He has made everything beautiful in its time.
He has also set eternity in the human heart;
yet no one can fathom what God has
done from beginning to end.

ECCLESIASTES 3:11 NIV

It is not opinions that man needs; it is truth. It is not theology; it is God. It is not religion; it is Christ. It is not literature and science; but the knowledge of the free love of God and His only-begotten Son.

Horatius Bonar

DaySpring

For more
inspiration,
scan here:

Release your burdens to Jesus and you will never regret it! I'm praying you experience His true compassion and hope today.

As a father shows compassion to his children, so the LORD shows compassion to those who fear him.

PSALM 103:13 ESV

If I can remember to turn my burdens over to Him every day, the whole day goes a lot better.

Johnny Cash

All our hurts, questions, fears, and joys find their home in Jesus. I'm praying you find great comfort in Him and experience His life-changing love.

God is *my strength* and *power,*
and He makes my way perfect.

II SAMUEL 22:33 NKJV

How do we know that God cares? Because Jesus. How do we know good will ultimately overcome bad? Because Jesus. How can we live with hope in our hearts and dancing in our feet, even when times get tough? Because Jesus.

Keion Jackson

Fear not, friend. Instead, ask God to take your fears and give you peace in return. I'm praying you find deep and lasting peace today.

"Fear not, for I am with you;
be not dismayed, for I am your God.
I will strengthen you, yes, I will help you,
I will uphold you with My righteous right hand."

ISAIAH 41:10 NKJV

Peace doesn't mean that you will not have problems.
Peace means that your problems will not have you.

Tony Evans

DaySpring

For more inspiration, scan here:

If you haven't felt God's lavish love before, then I'm praying you do, with my whole heart! His love changes everything.

How great is the goodness You have stored up for those who fear You. You lavish it on those who come to You for protection, blessing them before the watching world.

PSALM 31:19 NLT

How long and high and deep and wide is the love of Jesus.

Trieste Vaillancourt

DaySpring

For more inspiration, scan here:

Your life has great value to God and to this world. I'm praying you see the fulfillment of that purpose soon.

I thank my God upon
every remembrance of you.

PHILIPPIANS 1:3 NKJV

God put you on the journey.
You are not here by chance or accident;
you are here because God put you here.
Long before the world was created God knew all about you,
and He planned to give you life.
From all eternity you were part of His plan.

Billy Graham

DaySpring

For more inspiration, scan here:

When the joy of Jesus is present, it outweighs every pain and troubling circumstance. I'm praying for deep and lasting joy to fill your heart today.

The joy of the L*ORD* *is your strength.*

NEHEMIAH 8:10 NIV

He is no fool who gives what he cannot keep to gain what he cannot lose.

Jim Elliot

The good news is, Jesus never leaves us. He never gives up on us. He always shows up when we call, and He will continue His work in us till the end. Praying for you.

I am certain that God, who began the good work within you, will continue His work until it is finally finished on the day when Christ Jesus returns.

PHILIPPIANS 1:6 NLT

When we believe and walk in the light of God's trustworthiness, we can hardly miss finding Him to be so.

Ruth Chou Simons

God loves you beyond measure. Jesus longs to bring you into the presence of such deep and redeeming love. I'm praying your heart finds rest with Him today.

For You created my inmost being; You knit me together in my mother's womb. I praise You because I am fearfully and wonderfully made; Your works are wonderful, I know that full well.

PSALM 139:13–14 NIV

God is okay with me even when I'm not okay with me.

Lysa TerKuerst

DaySpring

For more inspiration, scan here:

God isn't afraid of questions or doubts. In fact, He wants you to confide in Him and trust Him to answer with love and grace. I'm praying you find peace through His heart today.

"The thief comes only to steal and kill and destroy. I came that they may have life and have it abundantly"

JOHN 10:10 ESV

Jesus didn't come to tell us the answers to the questions of life; He came to be the answer.

Timothy Keller

Every time we trust God with our prayers, He is filled with love and compassion for us. I'm praying you sense His love today and find answers where your heart needs them most.

But if . . . you seek the L*ORD your God,*
you will find Him if you seek Him
with all your heart and with all your soul.
DEUTERONOMY 4:29 NIV

There is no way to learn to pray but by praying.
Samuel Chadwick

Today I'm asking that God would help you to see yourself the way He sees you. Beautiful. Worthy. Delightful.

"You are precious and honored in My sight, and . . . I love you."

ISAIAH 43:4 NIV

When I say that I long for unconditional love, God says, "You are My beloved."

Renee Swope

I'm praying for you today as you face what you're facing. I'm asking God to encourage you and give you all you need to get through.

We love each other because He loved us first.

I JOHN 4:19 NLT

There is only one secure foundation: a genuine,
deep relationship with Jesus Christ,
which will carry you through any and all turmoil.
No matter what storms are raging all around,
you'll stand firm if you stand on His love.

Charles Stanley

DaySpring

For more inspiration, scan here:

God can overwhelm you with what He can and wants to do in your life. I'm praying for you to experience this firsthand!

The LORD has done great things for us, and we are filled with joy.

PSALM 126:3 NIV

No one can be saved in virtue of what he can do. Everyone can be saved in virtue of what God can do.

Karl Barth

I'm asking God to give you His courage. It's a game changer. A very big deal, in a very good way.

Be strong and courageous.
Do not fear or be in dread of them,
for it is the Lord your God who goes with you.
He will not leave you or forsake you.

DEUTERONOMY 31:6 ESV

Courage is contagious.
When a brave man takes a stand,
the spines of others are often stiffened.

Billy Graham

I'm asking God to show you His heart for you, through your dreams and talents and hopes come to life. You are meant to shine!

"All things are possible with God."

MARK 10:27 NIV

God has a dream for you, your talents, your one life that never has been and never will be duplicated by anyone else.

Holley Gerth

For more
inspiration,
scan here:

May you always find Jesus in your boat, in every storm. He wants to be there, and He longs to get you through, right by His side.

Now may the Lord of peace Himself give you peace at all times and in every way.

II THESSALONIANS 3:16 NIV

Peace doesn't come from finding a lake with no storms. It comes from having Jesus in the boat.

John Ortberg

For more inspiration, scan here:

With Jesus, there is no reason to fear. NONE. Because He's seen the end of the story, and has, in fact, written the ending with victory and hope. I'm praying you find the courage to believe Him.

"Behold, I am with you always, to the end of the age."

MATTHEW 28:20 ESV

There is never a reason to lose hope. Jesus says, "I am with you until the end of the world."

Pope Francis

I'm praying for you to choose hope. Because there is no greater gift than to get to trust the One who gave up everything so that we could have it all.

He gave up His divine privileges; He took the humble position of a slave and was born as a human being. When He appeared in human form, He humbled Himself in obedience to God and died a criminal's death on a cross. Therefore, God elevated Him to the place of highest honor and gave Him the name above all other names.

PHILIPPIANS 2:7–9 NLT

Jesus is God spelling Himself out
in language that men understand.

S.D. Gordon

I'm praying you feel God's nearness, hope, compassion, and love today. His love is life changing!

"Never will I leave you;
never will I forsake you."

HEBREWS 13:5 NIV

God loves us with an everlasting love;
He is our Refuge when we are weak,
our Helper when we cannot cope.

Elisabeth Elliot

DaySpring

For more inspiration, scan here:

I'm praying for you today, asking God to make His undeniable, overwhelming, personal love evident to you beyond a shadow of a doubt.

For I am persuaded that neither death nor life,
nor angels nor principalities nor powers,
nor things present nor things to come,
nor height nor depth, nor any other created
thing, shall be able to separate us from the love
of God which is in Christ Jesus our Lord.

ROMANS 8:38–39 NKJV

If I could, I would bottle up hope and give it to everyone in the world because hope changes everything.

Maghon Taylor

For more inspiration, scan here:

I'm asking God to give you the wisdom you need to make this tough decision.

The Lord is my strength and my shield;
in him my heart trusts.

PSALM 28:7 ESV

Take one day at a time.
Today, after all, is the tomorrow
you worried about yesterday.

Billy Graham

DaySpring

For more
inspiration,
scan here:

Submit your cares and concerns to God. He will hold them, and you, so gently. I'm praying you feel wrapped in His love.

No power in the sky above or in the earth below—indeed, nothing in all creation will ever be able to separate us from the love of God that is revealed in Christ Jesus our Lord.

ROMANS 8:39 NLT

Trust God. He will most certainly care for you.

Candace Cameron Bure

DaySpring

For more
inspiration,
scan here:

May you encounter the Redeemer, the Healer, the Savior, the Prince of Peace, and the Bearer of Hope, in all the ways you need Him. Praying for you!

Thanks be to God for His indescribable gift!

II CORINTHIANS 9:15 NIV

It is good to be tired and wearied by the futile search after the true good, that we may stretch out our arms to the Redeemer.

Blaise Pascal

For more
inspiration,
scan here:

You were made in the image of God, which means you bear the marks of royalty. I'm praying you understand the depth of that truth. There is no higher honor!

For we are His workmanship, created in Christ Jesus for good works, which God prepared beforehand that we should walk in them.

EPHESIANS 2:10 NKJV

Life is about Jesus.
We are not here to tell our story, but His.

Francis Chan

DaySpring

For more
inspiration,
scan here:

I'm asking God to watch over you today. You can trust this: He is who He says He is.

"I am the vine; you are the branches.
Whoever abides in me and I in him,
he it is that bears much fruit,
for apart from me you can do nothing."

JOHN 15:5 ESV

In the midst of your battles,
never forget that God loves you
and He has a plan for you.

Joyce Meyer

No one else in all of history can say they have kept every one of their promises. God has, and is, and He wants you to experience the fulfillment of every promise. I'm praying you do!

[God] has given us great and precious promises. These are the promises that enable you to share His divine nature.

II PETER 1:4 NLT

We know our best is ahead of us, so may we run forth, releasing all that is behind.

Cleere Cherry Reaves

I'm praying you'll experience God's peace today.

Glory to God in the highest heaven,
and on earth peace to those
on whom His favor rests.

LUKE 2:14 NIV

The peace of Jesus can't be stolen or destroyed.
We don't need to ask for it
because it's already ours.
Peace is a gift, and all we have to do is say "yes."

Trieste Vaillancourt

DaySpring

For more
inspiration,
scan here:

God loves you. He really, truly, does, like no one has before or ever will. I'm praying you know that to be true today and every day.

In this the love of God was manifested toward us, that God has sent His only begotten Son into the world, that we might live through Him.

1 JOHN 4:9 NKJV

God proved His love on the cross. When Christ hung, and bled, and died, it was God saying to the world, "I love you."

Billy Graham

No one is more trustworthy than God because He will never let you down. I'm praying that as you trust Him with the unknown, your faith will grow.

God is the one who saves me; I will trust Him and not be afraid. The Lord, the LORD *gives me strength and makes me sing. He has saved me."*

ISAIAH 12:2 NCV

Trust whatever [God] has for you. It will be better than anything you can plan for yourself.

Francis Chan

DaySpring

For more inspiration, scan here: